Mama Mudbug's
Look Book

To
Seth
& love you,
Mama Jeanne
10/14/23
This is from
Echo Bluff
in Missouri!

MAMA MUDBUG'S LOOK Book

A Young Explorer's Guide to Critters of the Missouri Ozarks

written and illustrated by JANET PRICE

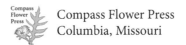

Compass
Flower
Press

Compass Flower Press
Columbia, Missouri

Published by
Compass Flower Press
Columbia, Missouri

Library of Congress Control Number: 2022920447
ISBN: 978-1-951960-37-7

This book is dedicated to:

My husband Roger, who made this book really happen.

My father, who taught me how to draw.

My mother, who encourages me in all of my crazy endeavors.

Special thanks to my niece Maggie for the wonderful cover art, and to my family for sharing opinions that were so valuable.

For Libby

Note from the Author:

This is not your typical field guide! Even little kids who can't read can look at these pictures and say, "That's it!"

Most of these animals are common to the Ozarks. Some are not so common, but you'll know 'em when you see 'em! (See Hercules Beetle, for example.)

If you want scientific names, range maps or technical terms, you can find those in a million other field guides already on the shelves.

If you want large, clear pictures of critters to help your kids identify what they see in the Missouri Ozarks, then you've come to the right place.

This is an exploration guide, with activities to encourage observations in nature. These fun facts may spark your interest, so go outside to see more stuff I didn't point out! Some things may seem too strange to be true, but they are strange *and* true. You can't make this stuff up!

Suggestion: Bring along a journal or paper and colored pencils when you are exploring. Draw or write what you see, hear, smell, or touch, and how it makes you feel. What great memories you can keep forever!

There are so many cool critters out there! These are just a few to get you started. Free exploration in nature is good for you, and so is dirt! Yes, really! Above all, explore and have fun! So much more is out there, if you just l(◉◉)k !

To my naturalist friends: I maintained a degree of accuracy in the drawings for this work, but my main goal is ease of recognition with the focus on identifying features, so the number of legs or wings is correct, but the number of segments in a leg or wing venation may not be.

MAMA

MUDBUG

Tips to remember from Mama Mudbug

 points out key identifying features of the animal.

 shows things to seek out in your explorations outdoors.

 is a warning to handle with care OR not handle at all!

 encourages interaction with nature.

 means check the appendix for more information or fun facts.

GRASSHOPPER

Did you know I have wings and can fly?

L👀K FOR the brown "tobacco juice" I spit on your hand.

CRICKET

I can bring good luck!

NOT a stinger; I lay my eggs with this.

Some people eat me!

2

KATYDID

I look like a leaf!

TRY IT!
Listen for all my songs:
Katy-did
Katy-did-did-did
Katy....

Appendix
page 57

LOOK OUT!
We might pinch or bite.

PRAYING MANTIS

I can turn my head and look right at you!

I hold my "hands" like I'm praying.

3

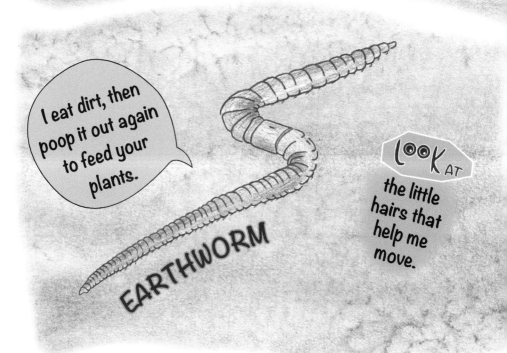

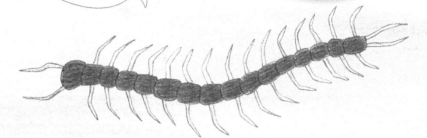

CENTIPEDE

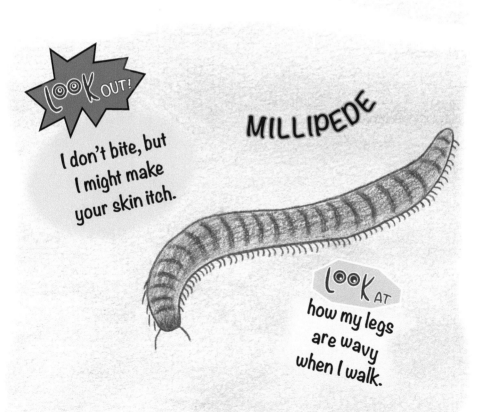

MILLIPEDE

LOOK AT my eyes on long stalks I can pull in.

Am I a snail without a shell?

SLUG

I do have a thin shell you can't see. Fooled ya?

LOOK FOR slime trails on the sidewalk.

SNAIL

TRY IT! Shine a flashlight behind me and watch my heart beat.

TRY IT! Put me on the window and watch my "foot" move.

Appendix page 59

6

TICK

My babies are called "seed ticks." They are tiny, like a period.

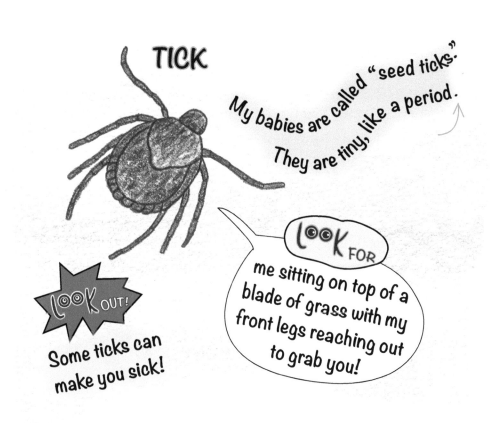

LOOK OUT!
Some ticks can make you sick!

LOOK FOR
me sitting on top of a blade of grass with my front legs reaching out to grab you!

VELVET MITE

LOOK AT
how velvety soft I am.

I'm not much bigger than a period.

LOOK FOR
me hitching a ride on daddy longlegs.

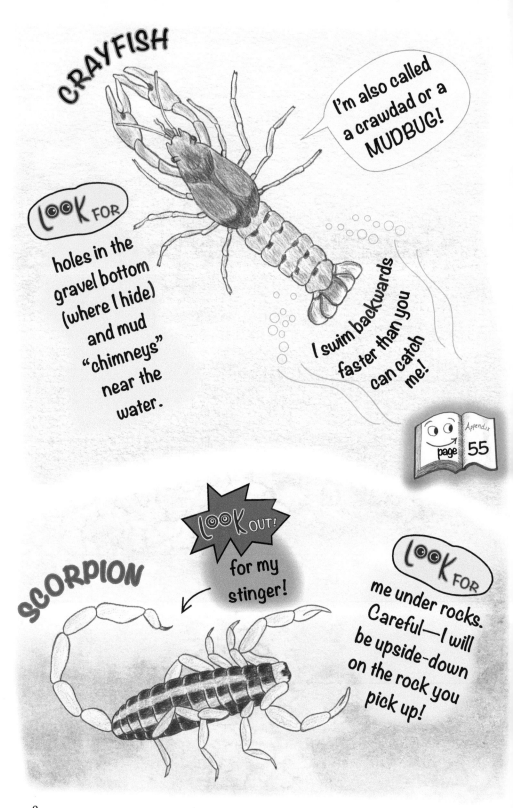

CRAYFISH

I'm also called a crawdad or a MUDBUG!

LOOK FOR holes in the gravel bottom (where I hide) and mud "chimneys" near the water.

I swim backwards faster than you can catch me!

page 55 Appendix

LOOK OUT! for my stinger!

SCORPION

LOOK FOR me under rocks. Careful—I will be upside-down on the rock you pick up!

SPITTLEBUG

Baby

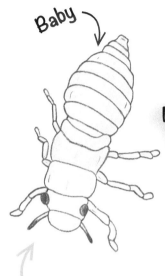

I hide in here.

 FOR

my bubbly "spit."

This turns into this:

TRY IT!

Run your finger gently through the bubbles to find me as a baby.

FROGHOPPER

Watch how I move.

Can you see how I got my name?

page 59

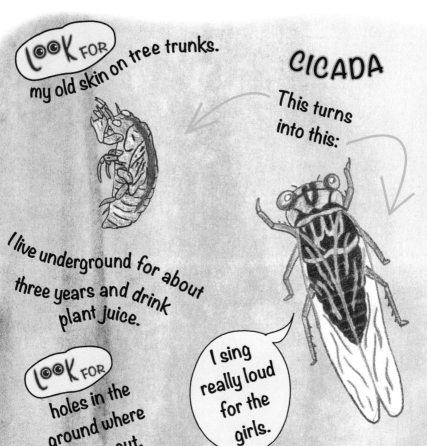

STINK BUG

I can drop stink bombs to defend myself.

My mouth is like a straw to suck up plant juices.

LOOK FOR me under and inside rotting wood.

I'm one of the good guys! I live outside!

WOOD ROACH

page 61

ASSASSIN BUG

LOOK OUT! for my beak!

My beak is like a needle with "killer spit" —but only to bugs.

page 52

11

ANTLION

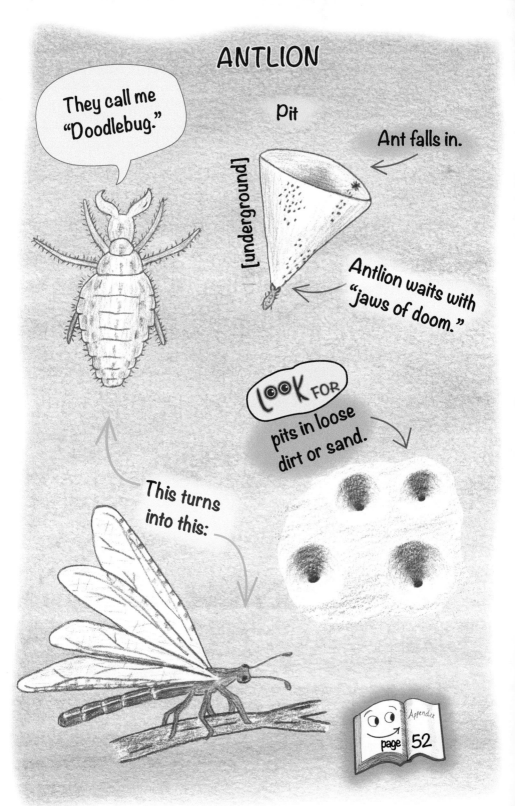

They call me "Doodlebug."

pit

Ant falls in.

[underground]

Antlion waits with "jaws of doom."

LOOK FOR pits in loose dirt or sand.

This turns into this:

Appendix

page 52

13

WATER STRIDER

I can walk on water. For real!

We make ripples to talk to each other.

 shadows and dimples on the water to find me.

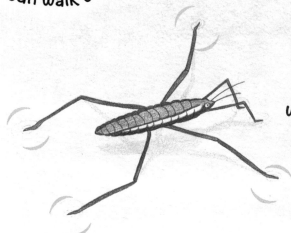

page 60

CRANE FLY

I fly wobbly.

I'm not a giant mosquito.

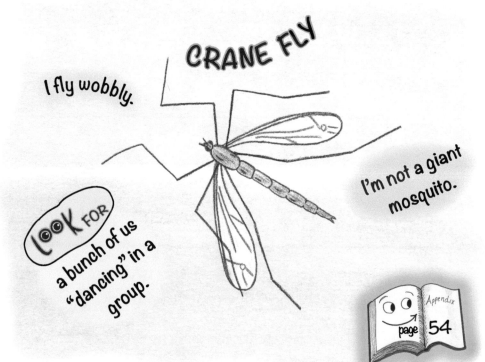

a bunch of us "dancing" in a group.

page 54

HOUSE FLY

I can walk upside-down on the ceiling. Can you?

I do not bite with this. I spit and suck. Ooh, yuck!

I help make flowers grow, so be nice to me.

MOSQUITO

LOOK OUT!

I bite with this!

My baby "wrigglers" hang upside-down in puddles and breathe through their rumps!

Appendix

page 58

DOBSONFLY

LOOK OUT!

I bite!

HELLGRAMMITE
DOBSONFLY LARVA

Harmless

This turns into this:

LOOK FOR

white spots (egg cases) on rocks near the water.

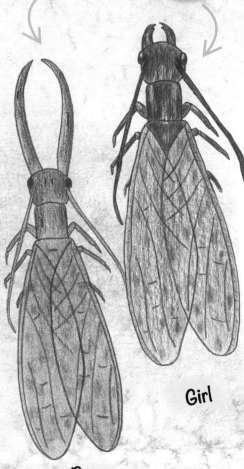

Girl

Boy

I fly really wobbly.

Before the eggs hatched, this looked like a bird poop **SPLAT** on a rock.

Appendix page 55

16

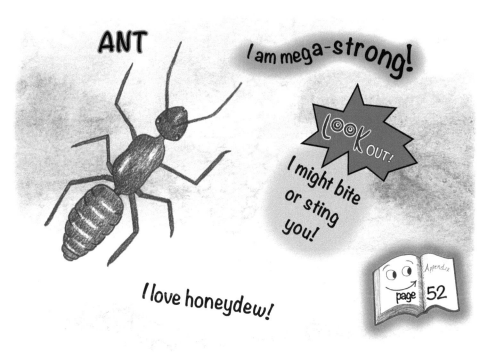

HONEYBEE

for my stinger — it only works once, but it hurts!

My wax honeycomb is full of sweet "bee spit."

page 56

BUMBLEBEE

My stinger is is back here.

My wings beat faster than a hummingbird's!

My "honeypot" is made of wax and is full of honey for my babies.

page 54

YELLOWJACKET

I have four wings and I'm a wasp.

LOOK OUT!

I sting!

Can I have some of your baloney sandwich and soda pop?

My paper nest is underground.

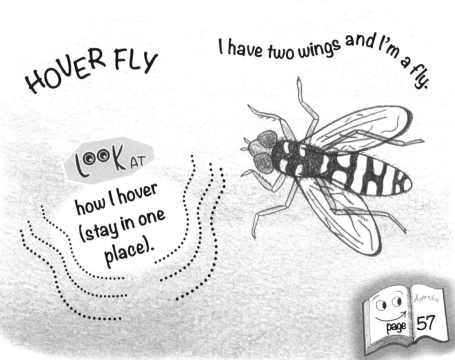

HOVER FLY

I have two wings and I'm a fly.

LOOK AT

how I hover (stay in one place).

page 57 Appendix

BALD-FACED HORNET

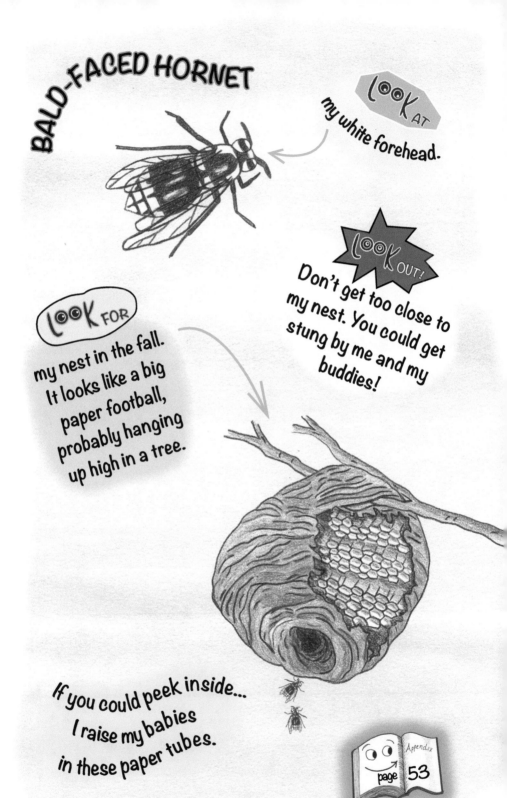

LOOK AT my white forehead.

LOOK OUT! Don't get too close to my nest. You could get stung by me and my buddies!

LOOK FOR my nest in the fall. It looks like a big paper football, probably hanging up high in a tree.

If you could peek inside... I raise my babies in these paper tubes.

Appendix
page 53

21

JAPANESE BEETLE

LOOK FOR
the skeleton
of a leaf
after I eat
all the good
parts.

LOOK AT
the white
tufts on
my sides.

JUNE BUG

King of the Crash Landing!

I'm attracted
to the light, but
too much will
kill me!

I crash into windows a lot. Don't ask me why.

Spoiler Alert: It's the light.

PINK LADYBUG

This turns into this:

Sometimes I'm this color.

I've always lived here. I'm a native!

page 59 Appendix

ASIAN LADYBUG
LADYBEETLE

This turns into this:

LOOK OUT!

I might bite!

LOOK AT

the "M" above my back.

I have sharp spines along my sides.

I'm new to the neighborhood. I'm originally from Asia.

page 52 Appendix

My jaws look scary, but I don't bite!

BESS BEETLE

TRY IT! If you hold me to your ear and rub me very gently, you can hear me squeeek.

Look how shiny I am!

CLICK BEETLE

Did my eyespots SCARE you?

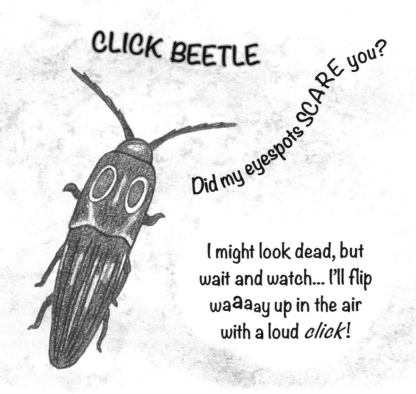

I might look dead, but wait and watch... I'll flip wa**aa**ay up in the air with a loud *click*!

LIGHTNING BUG
FIREFLY

L**OO**K AT
my glowing rump.

TRY IT!
Flash your light the same way I do and see if I come to you.

page 57 Appendix

HERCULES BEETLE

L**OO**K OUT!
I can pinch with these big horns!

L**OO**K AT
my horns! They are good for wrestling with the other boys.

I am really BIG and Super Strong!

page 56 Appendix

MOURNING CLOAK

I'm the first butterfly to come out in the spring.
Sometimes I look pretty shabby.
Winters are hard on me!

page 58

LOOK AT
my silvery
spots.

CLOUDLESS SULPHUR

I have big green eyes.

I'm so bright yellow, you can't miss me!

BLACK SWALLOWTAIL

Tails

LOOK FOR my caterpillar on parsley and wild carrot flowers.

RED-SPOTTED PURPLE

No tails!

This is me as a baby. I look like bird poop! Talk about safe — no one wants to eat me!

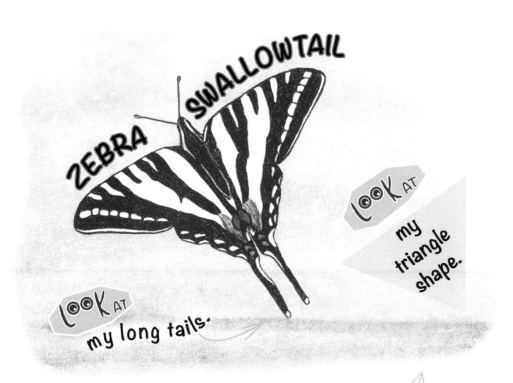

How do you think we got our names?

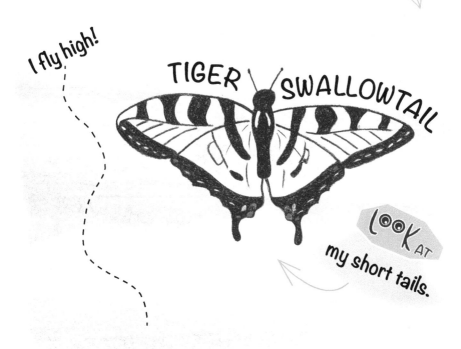

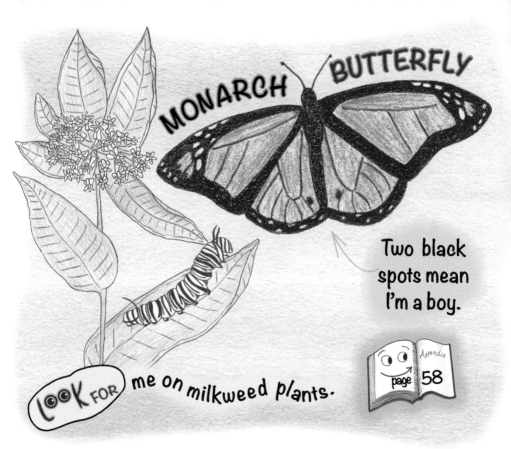

MONARCH BUTTERFLY

Two black
spots mean
I'm a boy.

Appendix
page 58

LOOK FOR me on milkweed plants.

VICEROY BUTTERFLY

LOOK AT

my two
curved black
lines on my
inner wings.

I glide more than a monarch.

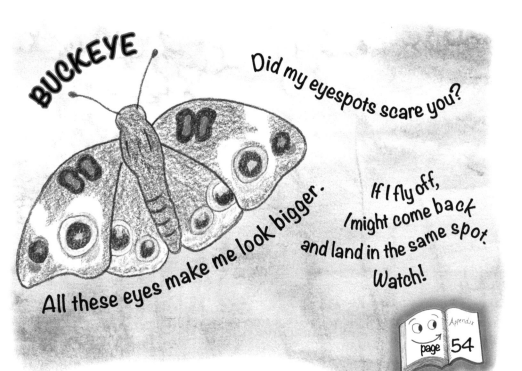

BUCKEYE

Did my eyespots scare you?

All these eyes make me look bigger.

If I fly off,
I might come back
and land in the same spot.
Watch!

page 54 Appendix

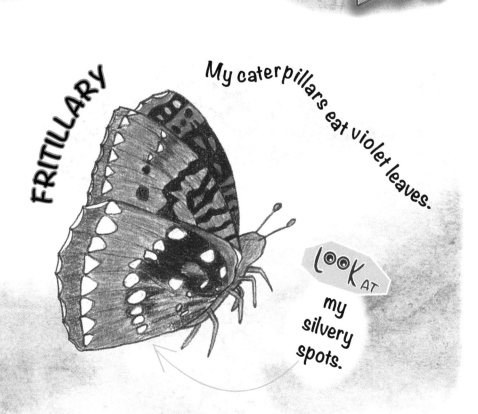

FRITILLARY

My caterpillars eat violet leaves.

LOOK AT
my
silvery
spots.

31

EASTERN-TAILED BLUE

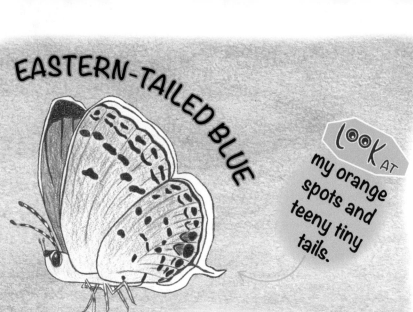

Look AT my orange spots and teeny tiny tails.

I am really small and fly close to the grass.

SILVER-SPOTTED SKIPPER

Look AT my big silvery spot.

I fly down low, like I'm skipping.

WOOLLY BEAR

This turns into this:

ISABELLA TIGER MOTH

LOOK OUT!
My hairs might make your skin itch.

page 61
Appendix

TENT CATERPILLAR

like a tent.

tucked close to the trunk

LOOK FOR my web

WEBWORM

on the branches like a spider web.

waaay out

LOOK FOR my messy web

LOOK FOR

my cocoon hanging from a branch or wrapped in a leaf on the ground.

POLYPHEMUS MOTH

My "evil eye" spots look SCARY!

page 59 Appendix

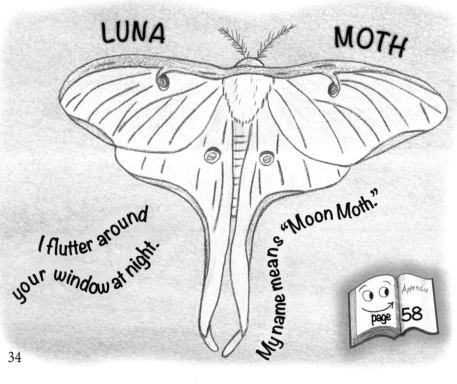

LUNA MOTH

I flutter around your window at night.

My name means "Moon Moth."

page 58 Appendix

34

REGAL MOTH

I only look <u>look</u> scary!

This turns into this:

HICKORY HORNED DEVIL

I'm as big as a hot dog!

IMPERIAL MOTH

Girls are bigger and more yellow than boys.

I don't have a mouth at all, so I can't eat as an adult.

page 57 Appendix

35

BROWN RECLUSE

LOOK AT the fiddle shape on my back.

LOOK OUT!

My bite can be dangerous.

I hide in piles of dirty clothes and papers and stuff, so keep your room neat!

Appendix page 54

BLACK WIDOW

LOOK AT my big shiny black rump with red marks.

Top

LOOK OUT!

My bite can make you sick.

Girls are round and shiny.

Underneath

Boys are brown and tiny.

Appendix page 53

36

JUMPING SPIDER

I'm cute and fuzzy.

L👀K AT my BIG eyes!

TRY IT!
Wiggle your finger in front of me and I'll "put up my dukes" like a boxer!

L👀K AT my big flat back!

TRAPDOOR SPIDER

"Hold the door, please..."

TRY IT!
If you see me, follow me to my tunnel.

page Appendix 60

FISHING SPIDER

I carry my egg sac in my mouth.

It looks like a cottonball.

I look soft and velvety.

LOOK AT my really looooong legs!

FUNNEL WEB SPIDER

LOOK FOR my tornado-shaped funnel web.

LOOK AT my long web-spinners.

TRY IT!
Tap my web with a piece of grass to make me run out!

WOLF SPIDER

LOOK FOR babies on Mom's back.

I carry my egg sac on my behind.

I'm not a bit dangerous!

Appendix page 61

TARANTULA

LOOK OUT! I use my legs to brush hairs at you that make you itch!

I rarely bite, and my venom is mild anyway.

My super-hairy feet help me walk and climb.

39

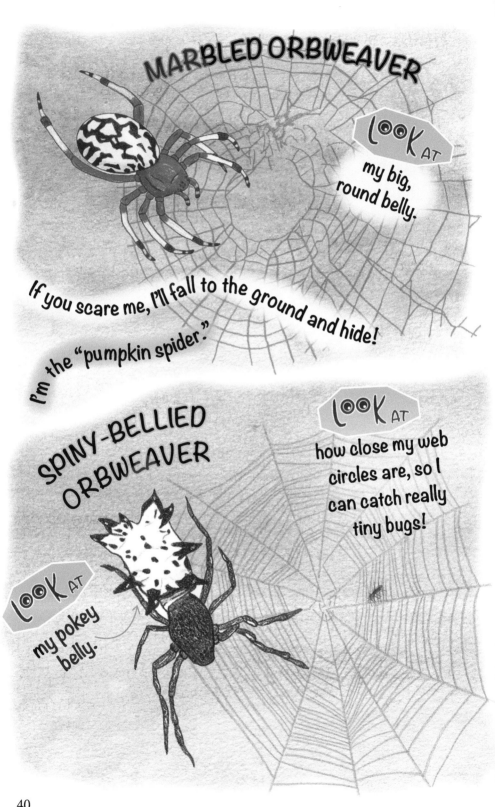

GARDEN SPIDER

TRY IT!
Watch me build my giant web in your doorway.

L**OO**K FOR
the zig-zag in the middle of my web.

page 56

ARROWHEAD ORBWEAVER

I'm the only one who sits in the web with my head up.

L**OO**K AT
how I sit with my legs tucked in.

I build my web across trails because that's where the bugs are!

41

CRAB SPIDER

I can change color (over several days) to match a flower.

LOOK AT how I hold my legs to the side like a crab. I can move in any direction like a crab, too!

DADDY LONGLEGS

Pssst — Wanna know a secret? I'm really NOT a spider!

LOOK AT my looong legs, like stilts.

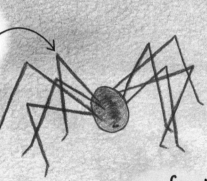

TRY IT! Wiggle your finger in front of me... I might wave back!

Appendix page 55

SPRING PEEPER

LOOK AT the X on my back.

Can you guess what sound I make in the spring? "PEEEP!"

My call is so loud it will hurt your ears!

CRICKET FROG

LOOK AT the triangle between my eyes.

TRY IT!
Click some stones together real fast to make my song.

43

45

RED-BACKED SALAMANDER

My legs are so short that my belly looks like it is dragging on the ground.

I have smooth skin.

FIVE-LINED SKINK

I have shiny scales.

Only babies have bright blue tails.
Adults are tan or brown.

page 56 Appendix

BLACK SNAKE

I can bite!

When I'm scared, I "buzz" my tail like a rattlesnake.

I am the Best. Climber. Ever!

page 53

FLYING SQUIRREL

LOOK AT my really BIG eyes.

I can't really fly. My skin flaps look like wings but work like a parachute.

TRY IT!

If you live near the woods, put out nuts or seeds at night and watch for us.

page 56

TURKEY VULTURE

LOOK FOR us circling up on hot air currents.

I fly pretty wobbly.

See how my wings are in a "V" when I fly?

Appendix page 60

BARRED OWL

LOOK FOR

wads of bone, fur or feathers under my favorite tree. Pellets are about the size of your thumb.

TRY IT!

Listen for me to call "Who cooks for you, who cooks for you-all?"

Appendix Pages

Alphabetical Listing of Fun Facts

American Toad *(page 44)*

Two big bumps (glands) behind the toad's eyes are full of a milky poison that tastes <u>really</u> bad! When another animal tries to eat the toad, it spits it out as fast as it can, and maybe even gets a little sick. Think it will try to eat a toad ever again?

Ant *(page 17)*

Ants love aphids because aphids drink plant juice and squirt it out their rumps. Ants eat it up like crazy! They even turn the aphids into zombies so they keep making the sweet "honeydew."

Antlion *(page 12)*

- Why *doodlebug*? Antlions *doodle* in the sand as they walk backwards, kinda like you doodle on your homework.
- You can't see it, but there's an antlion sitting at the bottom of that sand pit, with strong jaws sticking out. That ant crawling around the top just might fall in. Oh no, it's getting away! That antlion better do something quick! He uses his head like a shovel and throws sand up at that ant. When it slips down to the bottom, the antlion grabs it in his jaws and eats it. Yummm. Tasty. But wait for it… after the antlion sucks out the good stuff, he tosses the empty ant "skin" up out of the hole. Gotta keep the kitchen clean!

Asian Ladybug *(page 24)*

These ladybugs were sold to gardeners to control pests, but now, *they* are the pests!

Assassin Bug *(page 11)*

Assassin bug spit melts the bug's guts. Then it sucks up the guts while the bug is still alive! Slurrrp!

Bald-Faced Hornet *(page 20)*

- Bald-faced hornets won't bother you if you leave them alone and don't get too close to their football-shaped nest. That means DON'T squirt them with the hose!
- Adults mostly drink nectar from flowers, but they will also eat insects and spiders. They chew them up and feed them to their babies.

Black Snake *(page 49)*

When a black snake gets scared, it shakes its tail so fast that it makes noise. It sounds a lot like a rattlesnake, especially if it's in dry leaves. Lots of snakes can "buzz" their tail like that. What a great way to scare off an attacker!

Black Widow *(page 36)*

Black widows don't want to bite you. If one did, it would probably make you feel like you had the flu—and *that's* no fun. So if you find one, just stand back and be amazed with how cool it is.

Box Turtle *(page 47)*

- Why do you think they call it a "box" turtle? Because it can close up its shell tight, like a box. Really tight, so it is protected from dogs and coyotes and things that want to eat it.
- Box turtles love to live in the woods. But if you put them in your basement, they will get sick and die. So how about you leave them where you find them, OK?
- Box turtles can live to about fifty years old, if they don't get hit by a car. Help Mom and Dad watch for turtles on the road. Baby turtles are tiny (about the size of a quarter), so you have to watch close!

Brown Recluse *(page 36)*
If a brown recluse bites you, you probably wouldn't even notice. But... you might! And if you do, it might take a long time to heal. So just leave them alone, OK?

Buckeye *(page 31)*
Buckeye caterpillars eat plants that taste really bitter. That makes the caterpillar taste bad, too, so other things don't like to eat it.

Bumblebee *(page 18)*
How fast can you wave your arms? Well, bumblebees can move their wings so fast, the vibrations shake the pollen right out of the flowers. It's their super-power.

Carrion Beetle *(page 22)*
If you see a carrion beetle flying, you might think it's a bumblebee. Nature sure is tricky.

Copperhead *(page 48)*
If you get bit by a copperhead, you'll probably feel sick. Most people won't die from it. But don't test it! Be smart and just leave them alone!

Crane Fly *(page 14)*
- Adults feed on nectar from flowers or other plants.
- See all that wood and leaves and dead stuff rotting on the ground? Hmmm, I wonder why we don't see more of that laying around. Wait, I know—crane flies eat a lot of it! Whew. It sure would be a mess without them.

Crayfish *(page 8)*

Crayfish are really good fish bait. People eat them, too, sometimes out of a paper bag like popcorn. Do you?

Daddy Longlegs *(page 42)*

- The body of a daddy longlegs is just a blob with loooong skinny legs. Can you see how that is different from a spider?
- A daddy longlegs can't hurt you! They don't have fangs or venom, so it couldn't bite even if it wanted to! Which it doesn't. So don't worry.
- In the fall, see if you can find a bunch of daddy longlegs hanging out in a clump. It looks like a living hairball.

Dobsonfly *(page 16)*

The boys have super-long pinchers that look really scary! Don't worry, though. They can't push hard enough to really hurt you with them. But look out for the girls! Their pinchers are short, but they will hurt!

Dung Beetle *(page 22)*

- There's a lot of food left in that poop pile! A dung beetle rolls it into a ball bigger than itself, uses its back legs to roll it home, buries it and lays eggs in it. When they hatch, they eat the poop for lunch! Gross to you, yummy to them!
- Some nights, a dung beetle will stand on top of its poop ball and just look up at the stars. That's how it finds its way home. No cell phone or map needed. Can you do that?

Five-Lined Skink *(page 46)*

Young skinks have bright blue tails. If an animal attacks it, the tail might fall off and wiggle, wiggle, wiggle. While the attacker watches the tail wiggling, the skink can run away!

Flying Squirrel *(page 49)*

Flying squirrels need lots of trees in their neighborhood, some with good holes (like old woodpecker holes) for the squirrels to nest in. Skydivers have made special suits with flaps like a flying squirrel, so they can glide through the air, too. (Don't try this at home!)

Garden Spider *(page 41)*

That zig-zag in the web is called a *stabilimentum*. Can you say that three times fast? Nobody knows for sure why garden spiders build it that way.

Green Darner *(page 13)*

- Green darners are fierce hunters and love mosquitoes! Their babies eat baby mosquitoes, too.
- Ever hear someone talk about a *katynipper*? If you live in the Ozarks, it was probably a Green Darner.

Hercules Beetle *(page 26)*

- Hercules beetles don't bite, but those big horns can give you a nasty pinch! So watch your fingers.
- When a Hercules beetle gets scared, it makes a huffing sound to scare off an attacker. It sure would scare me!

Honeybee *(page 18)*

Did you ever spit up just a little and make it into a bubble in your lips? I bet you have. Well, a honeybee will drink nectar, then spit some back up and make a tiny "bubble" in its mouth. His buddy bees fan their wings really fast, and the bubble gets thick and sticky. Mmmmm, honey!

Hover Fly *(page 19)*
What looks like a bee, buzzes like a bee and pokes its rump at you like a bee, but doesn't sting like a bee? A hoverfly, that's what!

Imperial Moth *(page 35)*
- Most of the big moths make cocoons but not the imperial moth. It buries itself in the soil, turns into a pupa, then uses its claws on its back end to dig its way out.
- Look at that maple or sycamore tree. Can you see the imperial moth sitting there? Probably not. It looks just like the leaves, so you might not see it until it flies away. Amimals that want to eat it can't see it very well either. Perfect disguise!
- When the caterpillar hatches from the egg, it swallows air and blows up like a balloon!

Jewelwing *(page 13)*
Jewelwings are the only damselflies with black wings. Boys may have prettier colors, but girls have the jewel. They talk to each other by snapping their wings together.

Katydid *(page 3)*
Listen for it. Can you hear the difference? Katydids sing really fast when it's hot and reeaally sloooow when it's cold outside.

Lightning Bug *(page 26)*
Boy lightning bugs flash a secret code to find a girlfriend, but sometimes the girl cheats. She'll flash someone else's code. Tthen when the boy comes close, she eats him! Sneaky trick, huh?

Luna Moth *(page 34)*

- Look at the luna moth antennae. Do they look like feathers? That's a boy. Yep, the boys' antennae are prettier than the girls'. They use these fancy antennae to know when the girls are calling them for a date.
- The luna moth's super-long tails make it hard for bats to find them and eat them.

Monarch Butterfly *(page 30)*

Monarchs are disappearing. You can help! Count monarchs or plant a monarch waystation. Look up "Monarch Watch" online to find out more.

Mosquito *(page 15)*

- Boy mosquitoes drink plant juices. Girls drink blood, and only when they get ready to lay their eggs. As the boys move from flower to flower, they spread pollen around. Now the flowers can make seeds to grow new flowers.
- Fish, birds, dragonflies and tons of other animals eat mosquitoes and their babies. So even though we don't like them, mosquitoes are important to have around!
- Bug zappers don't kill many mosquitoes because they are not attracted to lights, but they <u>do</u> kill a lot of moths and other "good" bugs. So <u>please</u> don't use them, OK?

Mourning Cloak *(page 27)*

Mourning means *sad*, just like these dark, dreary colors.

Mud Dauber *(page 21)*

- To build a nest, a mud dauber gets a mouthful of mud. (Ewww...) It makes little mudballs with mud and its own spit, then flies back to make its nest. It smears the mud out into a tube using its forehead. Works nicely, don't you think?

- Ever hear that people sing better in the shower? Mud dauber wasps "sing" when they work on their nest tubes. It sounds even louder when it echoes in the tube. The singing helps make the mud smoother. Get up close and listen. Does it sound kinda like bagpipes?
- Wanna try something really cool? Hold white paper under the mud nest tubes and break one open. See those spiders that fall out? They can't move, but they are still alive! The baby wasp will eat them when it hatches inside of the mud tube. Yummm.

Paper Wasp *(page 21)*
Paper wasps chew up wood and mix it with spit to make their nests.

Pink Ladybug *(page 24)*
Some wasps can turn pink ladybugs into zombies. Then the ladybugs have to take care of the wasp babies. Weird, huh?

Polyphemus Moth *(page 34)*
If something tries to eat a polyphemus caterpillar, it makes clicking sounds with its mouth, then pukes. Not so tasty anymore, right?

Snail *(page 6)*
Snails use a radula (like a tongue with tiny teeth) to scrape and eat plants. It feels like scraping a fingernail on your hand. Try it!

Spittlebug *(page 9)*
- A spittlebug sits upside down on a plant stem and drinks its juice. The juice squirts out of its butt, all bubbly. It flows down, covering the spittlebug like a blob of spit. What a disquise!
- Go ahead—stick your finger in the bubbles and gently look at the spittlebug. Don't forget to put it back when you're done!

Trapdoor Spider *(page 37)*

Did you ever play *Hide and Seek* and peek out of the closet? How about *Hide and Eat?* A trapdoor spider hides in a hole in the ground with a silk and dirt door. If a bug walks by, the spider opens the door, runs out, grabs it and eats it! The more it eats, the bigger it gets, so it has to keep making its door bigger, too. If you look up close, the door will look sort of like rings in a tree trunk.

Turkey Vulture *(page 50)*

Yes, turkey vultures eat dead stuff. Gross! But they like it freshly dead, not rotten. They're not uncivilized! Think about this for a minute: If vultures didn't eat it, all that dead, smelly stuff would be all over the place, making us sick! Say, "Thanks, Vultures!"

Water Strider *(page 14)*

- Water striders have hairs on their legs that let them skate on top of the water without falling in. They don't even get wet, because hair on their body keeps them totally dry. How cool is that?
- Baby mosquitoes hang right under the surface of the water. Guess who is there to eat them up? Yep, water striders. Striders Rock!

Watersnake *(page 48)*

Some fishermen complain that watersnakes eat the fish they want to catch, but it's not true. The snake is just too slow to catch those fish. It eats mostly other fish, frogs and tadpoles.

Widow Skimmer *(page 13)*

- Both boy and girl widow skimmers have big black marks on their wings close to the body. Boys also have big white patches.
- Dragonflies were around long before dinosaurs. Some had wings that spread as long as your arm! (But don't worry. Those giant ones aren't around anymore.)

Wolf Spider *(page 39)*

- Some wolf spiders are small and look like a funnel web spider but don't have the long web-spinners sticking out the back.
- Let's go hunting. Get a flashlight with a good strong beam. Hold it up near your eyes. Squat down low and shine it around across the grass at the edge of the woods (or in your own backyard). If you see two tiny green eyes shining back at you, that's a wolf spider! Follow the reflecting eyes until you find the spider. If the lights disappear, the spider turned around. Just wait, and it will turn back again. Then go find it!

Wood Roach *(page 11)*

Roaches have been around since long before the dinosaurs and haven't changed much at all. That means they were pretty much perfect from the start!

Woolly Bear *(page 33)*

Some people think if a woolly bear's rusty stripe is big, the next winter will be warm. But really, the bigger brown stripe means it is older and has been eating a lot, probably because the winter last year was warm.

Group Index

Crawlers and Hoppers

Dragonflies and Damselflies

Flies and Other Flying Things

Frogs and Toads

Lizards, Salamanders and Skinks

Critter	Length or Height	Page
American Toad	2 1/2 inch	**44**, 52, 64
Ant	1/16 inch	**17**, 52, 63
Antlion	1 1/2 inch	**12**, 52, 63
doodlebug (larva)	1/2 inch	**12**, 52
Arrowhead Orbweaver	3/8 inch	**41**, 65
Asian Ladybug	1/4 inch	**24**, 52, 62
Assassin Bug	1 inch	**11**, 52, 64
Bald-Faced Hornet	3/4 inch	**20**, 53, 62
Barred Owl	20 inch	**50**, 62
Bess Beetle	1 1/4 inch	**25**, 62
Black Snake	48 inch	**49**, 53, 65
Black Swallowtail	3 1/2 inch	**28**, 62
Black Widow	1/4 inch	**36**, 53, 65
Box Turtle	6 inch	**47**, 53, 65
Brown Recluse	1/4 inch	**36**, 54, 65
Buckeye	2 1/4 inch	**31**, 54, 62
Bullfrog	6 inch	**45**, 64
Bumblebee	3/4 inch	**18**, 54, 62
Carrion Beetle	3/4 inch	**22**, 54, 62
Centipede	1 1/2 inch	**5**, 63
Cicada	1 1/4 inch	**10**, 64
Click Beetle	1 inch	**25**, 62
Cloudless Sulphur	2 1/2 inch	**27**, 62
Copperhead	24 inch	**48**, 54, 65
Crab Spider	1/4 inch	**42**, 65
Crane Fly	1 1/2 inch	**14**, 54, 64
Crayfish	3 inch	**8**, 55, 65

INCH 1 2 3 4 5

Critter	Length or Height	Page
Jewelwing	2 inch	*13*, 57, 64
Jumping Spider	1/2 inch	*37*, 65
June Bug	1 inch	*23*, 62
Katydid	2 inch	*3*, 57, 64
Ladybug, Pink	1/4 inch	*24*, 62
Ladybug, Asian	1/4 inch	*24*, 62
Leopard Frog	2 1/2 inch	*45*, 64
Lightning Bug	1/2 inch	*26*, 57, 62
Luna Moth	4 inch	*34*, 58, 63
Marbled Orbweaver	3/4 inch	*40*, 65
Millipede	2 inch	*5*, 63
Monarch Butterfly	3 3/4 inch	*30*, 58, 63
Mosquito	1/4 inch	*15*, 58, 64
Mourning Cloak	3 inch	*27*, 58, 63
Mud Dauber	1 inch	*21*, 58-59, 62
Paper Wasp	1 inch	*21*, 59, 62
Pillbug	1/2 inch	*10*, 63
Pink Ladybug	1/4 inch	*24*, 59, 62
Polyphemus Moth	4 inch	*34*, 59, 63
Praying Mantis	2 1/2 inch	*3*, 64
Red-Backed Salamander	3 1/2 inch	*46*, 64
Red-Spotted Purple	3 inch	*28*, 63
Regal Moth	4 1/2 inch	*35*, 63
Scorpion	2 inch	*8*, 65
Silver-Spotted Skipper	2 inch	*32*, 63
Slug	2 inch	*6*, 63
Snail	1 inch	*6*, 59, 63
Spiny-Bellied Orbweaver	1/3 inch	*40*, 65

INCH 1 2 3 4 5

About the Author

Award-winning naturalist Janet Price has shared the wonder of the Ozarks with kids and families for over thirty years. After working with national, state, and county parks across the country, she currently volunteers with the Bonebrake Center of Nature and History in Salem, Missouri. Janet lives with her husband and their canine kids "way down yonder."

About the Cover Artist

Maggie Walsh specializes in communication and digital media design. Her award-winning work has graced covers of assorted publications for many years.

That's all there is.
There is no more.

Printed in the USA
CPSIA information can be obtained
at www.ICGtesting.com
JSHW041729150923
48472JS00001B/3